Viennaism

By Dave Minyard

Table of Contents

Viennaism 1

Forward 3

Chapter 1: "Dear Town of Vienna" 4

Chapter 2: What Vienna is actually like 8

Chapter 3: Dear Editor – lied to by Elected Officials 9

Chapter 4: Dear Editor – US Constitution does not apply here 10

Chapter 5: Additional sidewalks not the answer 11

Chapter 6: Additional sidewalks not the answer 12

Chapter 7: Neighbors sign petition opposing planned Vienna sidewalk project 14

Chapter 8: Fairfax County Times: Mixed public comment follows sidewalk proposals on opposite sides of the county 19

Chapter 9: What is "Viennaism"? 27

Chapter 10: Vienna evolving into totalitarian state 28

Chapter 11: Paul: comment 30

Chapter 12: 15 November 31

Chapter 13: 16 November 41

Chapter 14: 17 November 46

Chapter 15: 18 November 50

Chapter 16: In closing 51

Forward

There used to be a time, long, long ago where there was a town that had leadership that actually served the people they represented. We can't mention that name here because it is forgotten like the way those former servants of the people were back then. Viennaism has taken over, and like communism or totalitarianism, the leaders now serve their own interests. This is a book about what it has become.

Chapter 1: "Dear Town of Vienna"

Dear Town of Vienna

This includes Town Council

What happened to, "of the people, by the people, and for the people"? You obviously have forgotten that, unless you are outside the United States of America.

Did you know that if someone wants to close the street down for an event, they have to have everyone on the street sign a petition to agree to that, or the street cannot be closed. Hmmm, There are many who don't want sidewalks on Tazewell Road, NW. You obviously don't comply with "of the people, by the people, and for the people". Remember what you did the the residents on Alma Street, SE? Do you know after you breached your trust and put sidewalks in, that most of them moved out of Town? I guess that is your way of creating "Viennaism". You should be ashamed of yourselves.

The residents on Tazewell Rd, NW, Vienna, VA 22180

DO NOT SUPPORT SIDEWALKS and many others in Vienna don't

(and Alma Street, SE – remember them? Their petition?) , and we are the ones that are your "income", not the "street" you own, not the curbs or gutters, and not the grass you say is on your "right of way" that I cut (and you don't pay me for doing that). This is much like Communism where you think you rule and the peoples voice doesn't matter. Guess what. Elections will come and those who might still think there are people worth voting for, will be watching to find ways to vote you out. You've forgotten that you are there to support the residents, and not your own agenda. In the summer, you said you would not go forward with Tazewell because of the lack of support, and one Councilman even said to a resident here that if they voted for him, he would make sure the sidewalks wouldn't happen. Want to know who that is? Springsteen. There, now you know, and all of us know. I'm still "under the weather" and couldn't attend your "party" Monday night, but I hear others came, and a Resident from another area was extremely upset about your travesties to the hard working tax payers and residents of this regime controlled town. And like I said previously, I called Public Works 7 Oct 2022 with no return call. That is completely unacceptable. Please add this to your record as well as the attached letters to the editors.

It is inexcusable what you are doing. This town does not belong to you, yet you are treating it as such. What kind of elected officials do things like you are doing? Russia, China, North Korea. Ever heard of those places? You have made this Viennaism.

Chapter 2: What Vienna is actually like

What Vienna is actually like

Dear Editor,

Soon, WETA will do a story about Vienna, from the town of Vienna perspective, who's trying to sell you on the false reality of the town. The fact is, if you lived here, you'd have neighbors like mine who criminally trespass on your property without any consequences or charges, who throw trash in your yard, who harass you and your pets and yell obscenities in the middle of the night with no consequences or charges. This is what domestic terrorism looks like. Their visitors and service providers park on your side of the street the wrong way (which is illegal), and trespass on your property without any charges or consequences. That's what entitlement looks like. The politicians lie about not putting sidewalks in and then behind your back, go ahead with the plan to appease the few who actually run the game, when they could spend that money to help students with college funds. You can be singled out at a town event in front of many others and humiliated by town staff. You'll have speeders driving down your street and no one to address it because you're not in their circle. Meanwhile the special people have traffic calming devices on their streets. That's what living in Vienna is really like. Wanna live in a place like that? There's not a single organization in the town that hasn't, multiple times, received food, drink, etc. from me over the years, YEARS!! When there's water main breaks, I bring food and drinks. I even did that for the company that installed the new water line when on my street. When trash and recycling pickup comes, I throw mine in the truck to help. No one else does that. So this goes to show you what Vienna is really like - reality check from the "blue pill" they'll try to offer you.

Dave

Chapter 3: Dear Editor – lied to by Elected Officials

Dear Editor,

After being lied to by the Elected Officials in Vienna about sidewalks and their Staff not enforcing laws on the books on trespassing and abuse to animals and being harassed and threatened by people and no one arrested, and defamation of character committed by Staff with no one held accountable, I'd say to voting in Vienna, I'll pass. Elected Officials don't recognize the 1st Amendment of the Constitution of the United States and don't represent the interests of the people who voted them in before, so why? Why spend my time doing something that results in things like those things listed? Another Staff member said I'm 1/17,000 which was their way of humiliation and minimalizing me. Guess what? Many in this town feel this same way and you wouldn't let them speak either. So enjoy your cushy power over the people, your corruption, and your total disregard for honorable character and responsible governing that's suppose to be "of the people, by the people, and for the people" (Abraham Lincoln), not for your personal agendas.

Dave

Chapter 4: Dear Editor – US Constitution does not apply here

Dear Editor,

Apparently the US Constitution does not apply to one small town, where an enema called "Robert's Rules" was elevated above those who have been endowed with inalienable rights by God. Vienna, Va is that place. The very people who voted in those that put on the shelf, the 1st Amendment, and were not allowed 🚫 to speak 🎤 up at the misguided and poor financial choice of the elected officials. In fact, they lied 😬 because they said they would not move forward with installing of sidewalks on Tazewell Rd & changed their tune to move forward with it. So much for small town community where elected officials represent the very people who voted them in. That money should be better spent for scholarships for students which is another option but no, they want to put sidewalks on streets despite people walking on streets vs sidewalks where the street has sidewalks and they walk their dogs on the streets where there are sidewalks. You cannot justify this abhorrent exorbitant choice. What type of people are you trying to attract? Trespasser's? Animal abusers? Foul mouth domestic terrorists? Yea, that type came and live on Tazewell Rd and you didn't enforce laws on books. & their contractors stole electric and water from neighbors and were not arrested either. Such is the greed & arrogance here, & defamation of character your staff committed is also a crime. These reflect are the people you attract. Vision to reality - Dave

Chapter 5: Additional sidewalks not the answer

Letter: Additional sidewalk in Vienna is not the answer

Editor: I can see it now: more trash to report from residents and visitors of the rich people directly across the street who'll use sidewalks in front of my house as another form of entitlement.

Despite the size of theirs, residents and guests leave their garbage in my yard and on my side of the street, including cans, bottles (of alcoholic type and others), cigarettes and other trash from people devoid of decency. They park on my side of the street even though there's plenty of space on their side – another form of entitlement.

I refuse to support sidewalks on our street at all. It's a narrow street, to boot. I will never support a sidewalk on my side of the street.

Dave

Chapter 6: Additional sidewalks not the answer

Editor: I can see it now: more trash to report from residents and visitors of the rich people directly across the street who'll use sidewalks in front of my house as another form of entitlement.

Despite the size of theirs, residents and guests leave their garbage in my yard and on my side of the street, including cans, bottles (of alcoholic type and others), cigarettes and other trash from people devoid of decency. They park on my side of the street even though there's plenty of space on their side – another form of entitlement.

I refuse to support sidewalks on our street at all. It's a narrow street, to boot. I will never support a sidewalk on my side of the street.

Dave

Letter: Additional sidewalk in Vienna is not the answer

Chapter 7: Neighbors sign petition opposing planned Vienna sidewalk project

NEWS

Neighbors sign petition opposing planned Vienna sidewalk project

The Vienna Town Council advanced several sidewalk projects to a final engineering design phase last night (Monday), even as another project continues to draw strong opposition from residents on the affected street.

Nearly every resident on Alma Street Southeast has signed a petition opposing a proposed project to add a sidewalk on the even-numbered side of their street between Delano Drive SE and Follin Lane SE.

The town council authorized a contract with an engineering firm to conduct final design work on that project and three others on Oct. 11.

The initiative is funded by a $7 million charitable trust that former Councilmember Maud Robinson left after her death in 2019. Among other conditions, the trust money must be spent by fall 2024.

While several projects have moved forward this year, none have reached the construction stage yet, in part due to neighborhood opposition that evidently has not abated.

In addition to the Alma project, Sanders says his property will be affected by plans to add sidewalk on Delano Drive Southeast, from Echols Street to the end.

That project is among five that were approved for final engineering design yesterday:

- DeSale Street Southwest from Moore Avenue to Tapawingo Road and also to the end of the street
- Melody Lane Southwest from DeSale Street to Lullaby Lane
- Tazewell Road Northwest from Lawyers Road to Holmes Drive
- Orrin Street Southeast from Delano Drive to Follin Lane

The town said the cost to prepare those engineering design reports is $46,700, based on a proposal from Urban.

Tensions Rise over Public Input Process

A petition objecting to the project has garnered signatures from 10 of 12 residences on the street as of Sunday (Oct. 31). Resident Matt Sanders, whose property is on the corner of Alma and Delano, said he thinks the remaining homeowners will both oppose it.

Sanders tried to speak before the council's vote on Oct. 11, but in a brief exchange, Mayor Linda Colbert said it wasn't a public hearing.

"None of the residents on Alma and Delano have asked for or desire sidewalks. In fact they oppose it," Sanders said by email. "The council appears to be hell bent on spending this money and installing sidewalks whether their constituents want them. Just because this money is available, doesn't mean it has to be spent ramming sidewalks down the throats of residents."

Town Feels Urgency Over Trust Fund Deadline

The current wave of sidewalk projects, including the one on Alma Street, is part of a push by the Town of Vienna to speed up work on its Robinson Trust Sidewalk Initiative, which is intended to expand the town's sidewalk network.

Ahead of the Oct. 11 vote, Sanders said in a letter to the town that he could lose part of his driveway and a parking space to the sidewalk projects, stating that he may pursue legal action.

When he followed up on that letter before yesterday's meeting, Colbert told him that there would not be time for public comment, since a public hearing wasn't scheduled.

"We have a place on the agenda for comments from the public that are not on the agenda but sidewalks are on the agenda so it will not be allowed then either," Colbert wrote.

She also said the Department of Public Works has listened to residents' concerns and worked with them to achieve the best possible design for the neighborhood, telling Sanders to send comments for the council to council@viennava.com.

The Town of Vienna has posted video of last night's meeting, but as of press time, audio was not available for most of the public comment period. The town's information technology department said it would look into the matter.

Colbert acknowledged the audience later in the meeting.

"I know that a lot of you are here — probably all of you in the audience right now — for the sidewalks," the mayor said. "...[The] Town has to do the designs first and look at those sides of the street and see which one makes more sense, and then we'll have community input."

When another person tried to speak while she was talking, Colbert said public comment wasn't allowed at that time, because it would be unfair to people who weren't present.

"We're not ignoring you," she said, encouraging people to email the town council and adding the town's goal is to make the area as safe as possible for everyone.

Councilmember Nisha Patel asked about the status of sidewalk projects in the middle of town where they might be used more, requesting that the information be presented at a future public hearing.

Chapter 8: Fairfax County Times: Mixed public comment follows sidewalk proposals on opposite sides of the county

FEATURED

Mixed public comment follows sidewalk proposals on opposite sides of the county

By Collin Cope / Fairfax County Times

Collin Cope

Fairfax County Times

In an effort to improve safety and walkability for pedestrian traffic, officials in Fairfax County and the Town of Vienna are working towards the expanded construction of sidewalks in the county.

Two major proposals, however, receive differences in public comment and showcase stark contrasts in community attitudes regarding the perceived benefits or downsides to more sidewalks.

One of the proposals centers a section of land near Huntley Meadows Park and Hybla Valley Elementary School in Alexandria. Residents arguing in favor of this sidewalk spoke at an Oct. 11 Fairfax County Board of Supervisors meeting and highlighted a lack of pedestrian access to the park.

Times — FAIRFAX COUNTY

"Huntley Meadows Park, one of the few in Mount Vernon and Franconia districts, is currently not safely accessible by sidewalk," shared Mount Vernon District resident Cathy Hosek. "As a former resident of the Lafayette Apartments, located directly across the street from Huntley Meadows, I can assure you that the park is not easily accessible by any transportation mode, other than a car."

Given the benefit constituents receive from engaging in outdoor recreation, resident Liz Murphy emphasized the positives of access to pedestrian transportation, as well as public parks.

"Access to parks also improves community health and plays an important role for people seeking respite from the toll of the pandemic," said Murphy.

At the board meeting on Oct. 11, a proposal to incorporate funding for the construction of a sidewalk was heard without any public objection. The Board of Supervisors have not yet indicated whether they would provide funding for the sidewalks in Alexandria.

Fairfax County Times

Opposing opinions on sidewalks emerge in an isolated Vienna neighborhood, where residents strongly oppose the Vienna Town Council's recent proposals to introduce sidewalks on Tazewell Road Northwest, DeSale Street Southwest, Melody Lane Southwest and Orrin Street Southeast.

According to Vienna Mayor Linda Colbert, the safety and accessibility benefit to the construction of new sidewalks is clear and was always a part of the town's overall plan once funding became available.

"Thanks to a generous legacy bequest from the Robinson Family Trust, the Town is able to expedite its plan for a walkable community. Maud Robinson was a Vienna Town council member and her husband, Charles Robinson, was the Town mayor for 24 years. They loved Vienna and were active walkers all over town and understood the importance of sidewalks," said Colbert.

Fairfax County Times

Homeowners in this area express strong criticisms of this plan and feel their input was ignored by town officials. In an Oct. 10 Vienna Town Council meeting, members of the public were provided the opportunity to share their point of view.

"The bottom line is we do not want a sidewalk on our street. Please don't force one on us. Maud Robinson, God rest her saintly soul, would be mortified were she alive to see this playing out," said Tazewell resident, "She meant to bless people with something they want but can't afford. Not curse people with something they hate and can't avoid."

While many of these individuals are upset about a lack of input requested from them, their main concerns include a reduction in lawn space, an increase in pedestrian traffic, an impact on property aesthetics and the possibility of appropriating these funds more effectively. Residents also highlight the presence of recently constructed sidewalks on various nearby streets, such as Alma Street Southeast, as alternatives for pedestrians traveling through the neighborhood.

Fairfax County Times

Additionally, _____ claimed that the town of Vienna conducted a survey to gather public comment on the implementation of sidewalks, which received a majority disapproval from residents.

"Part of the reason I bought my house on Desale was because there were no sidewalks. That was part of the appeal. Imagine that," explained Desale resident

"We also have pollinator bees about 12-feet-in across 75 percent of the front yard," shared Tazewell resident _____ "I thought maybe the council could be a little more creative, perhaps maybe the balance of what it would cost to put sidewalks in on our street could go to a scholarship."

Fairfax County Times

Like most residents, Vienna resident   became aware of the proposal for sidewalks around late spring of 2020 and has been an active opponent to their construction. While he shares concerns most residents have, a major point of dissatisfaction for him is a disregard for public comment by the Town Council.

"People are concerned that elected officials have failed and breached their responsibilities to represent the people that pay their salaries. People are concerned with their personal lives being disrupted. People are concerned about the security of their homes and properties with unvetted contractors coming in. They reflect that the government is acting like communists and people are having to fight against tyranny,"

The mayor expressed in a comment that residents who had initially opposed sidewalk construction efforts eventually came around in support of them and felt community cooperation will ease this process.   (This is a lie. No one is changing their mind. Many have left the town and moved away because of this)

The mayor expressed in a comment that residents who had initially opposed sidewalk construction efforts eventually came around in support of them and felt community cooperation will ease this process.

(The following is a complete lie. Many have left the town because of this. No one has changed their mind)

"Some residents who initially resisted the sidewalk concept have expressed appreciation once sidewalks were completed in their neighborhood, and I hope others who are initially opposed to future projects will also come to appreciate the value of sidewalks," shared Colbert. "Achieving the vision of both the Town's Comprehensive Plan and Pedestrian Master Plan for a walkable community will require time, patience and collaboration between the town and residents."

Chapter 9: What is "Viennaism"?

What is "Viennaism?

Dear Editor,

Viennaism is synonymous with totalitarianism, or communism. But you don't have to travel to Russia or China to experience it. Just buy a house in the Gulag of Viennaism. Sure, the signs say, "Vienna", but that's false advertising. You become enslaved to the people who are supposed to represent you when in fact they represent their own interests. And your real estate taxes pay their salaries. You are their only bread and butter and they treat you how they want, as subjects of their kingdom. Take Reside on Alma Street, SE who all signed a petition against the sidewalks. Yet the Viennaism went ahead and put them in against their will. Most of them moved away from this evil empire of wretched people. Take this for an example of the Viennaism Council "Sprinkled and Dump on your yard" was walking his dog without a leash (against the law) and the dog did it's business on the property of a resident that opposes the sidewalks! Corruption! And he also lied because he said to that very resident that if they voted for him he would make sure the sidewalks wouldn't happen. So now you have your dog do it's business on a residence's property? So corrupt and evil. No sidewalks on Tazewell.

Dave

Chapter 10: Vienna evolving into totalitarian state

Letter: Vienna evolving into totalitarian state

Editor: What is "Viennaism"? It's synonymous with totalitarianism or communism. But you don't have to travel to Russia or China to experience it.

Just buy a house in the gulag of Viennaism. Sure, the signs say "Vienna," but that's false advertising. You become enslaved to the people who are supposed to represent you when in fact they represent their own interests.

And your real-estate taxes pay their salaries. You are their only bread and butter and they treat you how they want, as subjects of their kingdom. Residents on Alma Street, S.E., all signed a petition against installation of sidewalks. Yet the Viennaism went ahead and put them in against their will. Most of them moved away from this evil empire of wretched people.

And no sidewalks on Tazewell Road, N.W. We have many people who don't want sidewalks

Dave

Chapter 11: Paul: comment

Paul

I feel for you Dave. Older neighborhoods like these should be grandfathered in and not have to comply with rules like this. Vienna already has a problem with affordable housing and this will not help.

Chapter 12: 15 November

15 November 2022

Many of you, well town council, are patting yourself on the back for your so called victory last night. You hampered the right to free speech, you lied about the support for sidewalks on Tazewell, and you, as one council person put it, "rammed your sidewalks down our throat". You have reflected the very thing about politicians people have hated for years. You are self-serving, and don't care about the people who are responsible for the salaries of those who work for the town. One council person talked about growing up with sidewalks on his street. How ridiculous. So this is about you? Guess what, those in my household grew up with no sidewalks in front of most of the residences we lived in, and I have outperformed you in my life well more than you have in multiple lifetimes. Here is the fact – MOST THE PEOPLE ON TAZEWELL ARE OPPOSED TO YOUR SIDWALKS and considering your rambling about space on property, we the homeowners own most of the property on Tazewell, and your street makes up the minority. Oh guess what, you can't play ball on a sidewalk. You all have really made a spectacle of yourself with your arrogance. Your ego drives you. You dig for justifications to support your worthless objectives and think not of the people who live here and are the only things on this street that brings value – that's right, value!!!! You have taken me for granted for years, and I am not unaware of that. You have breached trust, and as such, your continue to show you do not care about those who you are supposed to be serving. You only serve the creature in the mirror you see. 15 Nov 2022 will go down in history at the very reality that this is Viennaism and not a town where freedom is honored by politicians who use their power for their own purpose. Despicable.

dave

15 November

It's USS Carr and USS Scranton day. Every 15 Nov since 15 Nov 2003 has been. It's a day I honor and give tribute to the men and women from the mighty warship an dthe boat I was aboard. Many thanks to Anthony Swain and Charles Melcher and their crews as well as VADM Fallon for my short and memorable TDY. The USS Carr provided an awesome lunch!!!! Hooyah!!!

DAVID MINYARD VISIT
SCHEDULE OF EVENTS
15 NOVEMBER 2003

Saturday, 15 November

1045	Arrive Naval Station Norfolk Tour and Information Center. Greeted by Lieutenant Junior Grade Dianna Kulik, USNR, COMFLTFORCOM Public Affairs Representative
1045-1100	Comfort Break
1100-1145	Windshield Tour on Naval Station Norfolk
1145-1200	Depart Tour and Information Center for lunch at Naval Station Galley
1200-1245	Lunch at Naval Station Galley
1245-1300	Depart Naval Station Galley en route Pier 3, Berth 4
1300-1430	Visit USS SCRANTON (SSN 756), greeted by Command Duty Officer
1430-1445	Depart Pier 3 en route Pier 10
1445-1545	Visit USS CARR (FFG 52), greeted by Command Duty Officer
1545-1600	Transit to Naval Station Norfolk Tour and Information Center. Lieutenant Junior Grade Kulik farewells guests

> Mr David Minyard and Family.
>
> Thank you for visiting our proud warship. Please enjoy your tour in USS Carr.
>
> Tony Swain
> Commanding Officer
> USS Carr FFG52

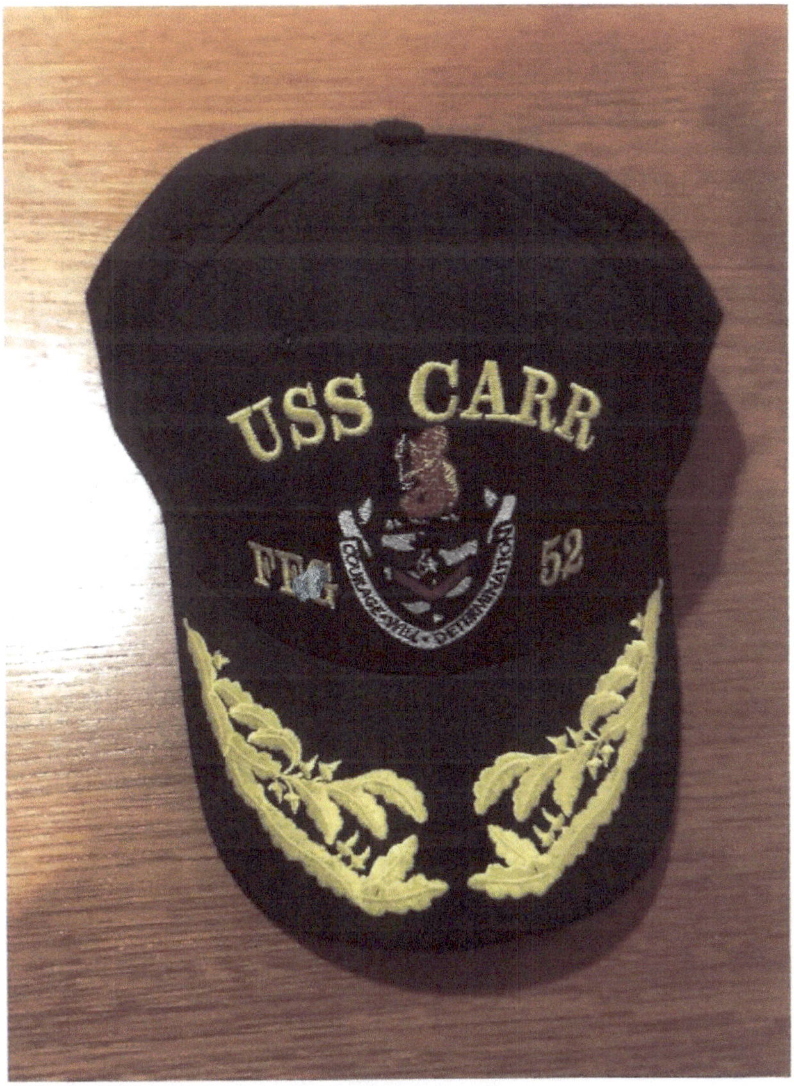
USS CARR
52

**WELCOME ABOARD
"IRON HORSE"
15 NOVEMBER 2003**

U.S.S. SCRANTON (SSN756)
Los Angeles-Class Attack Submarine

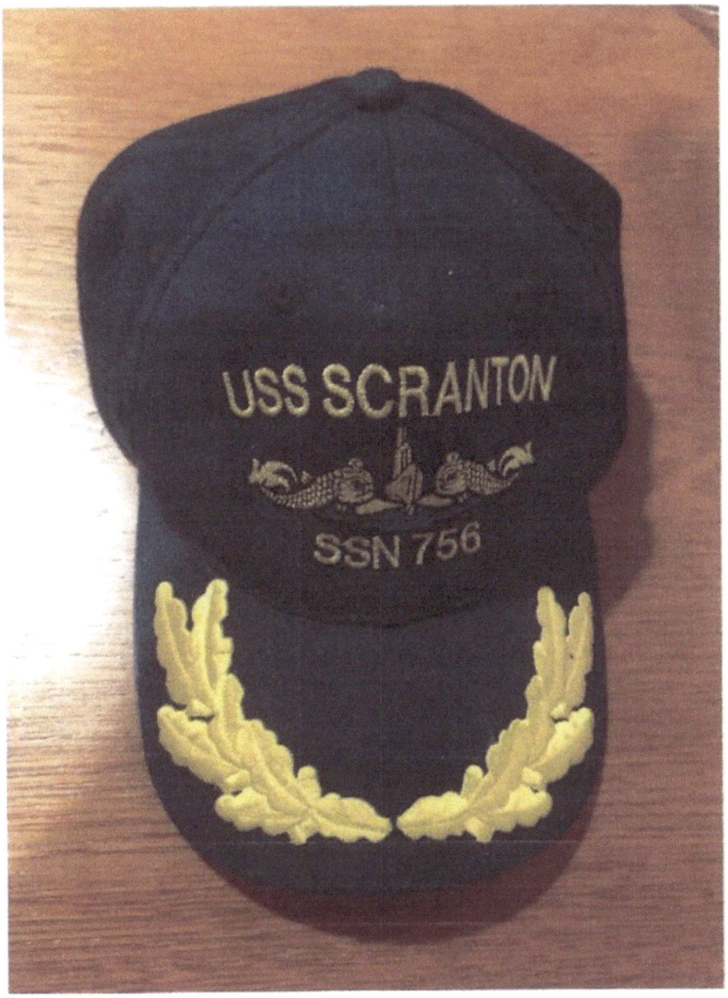
USS SCRANTON
SSN 756

Eagle's Watch Foundation
Providing Hope in Times of Need

Mr. David Minyard
Eagle's Watch Foundation

Dear Mr. Minyard,

I want to express my appreciation for the exceptional support you provide to our men and women in uniform. As a member of the America Supports You team, your organization helps strengthen the bonds between our military and the Americans they serve.

Thank you for letting service members and their families know how much their fellow Americans value their courage, commitment and sacrifice.

Sincerely,

Dave Minyard

www.eagleswatchfoundation.org

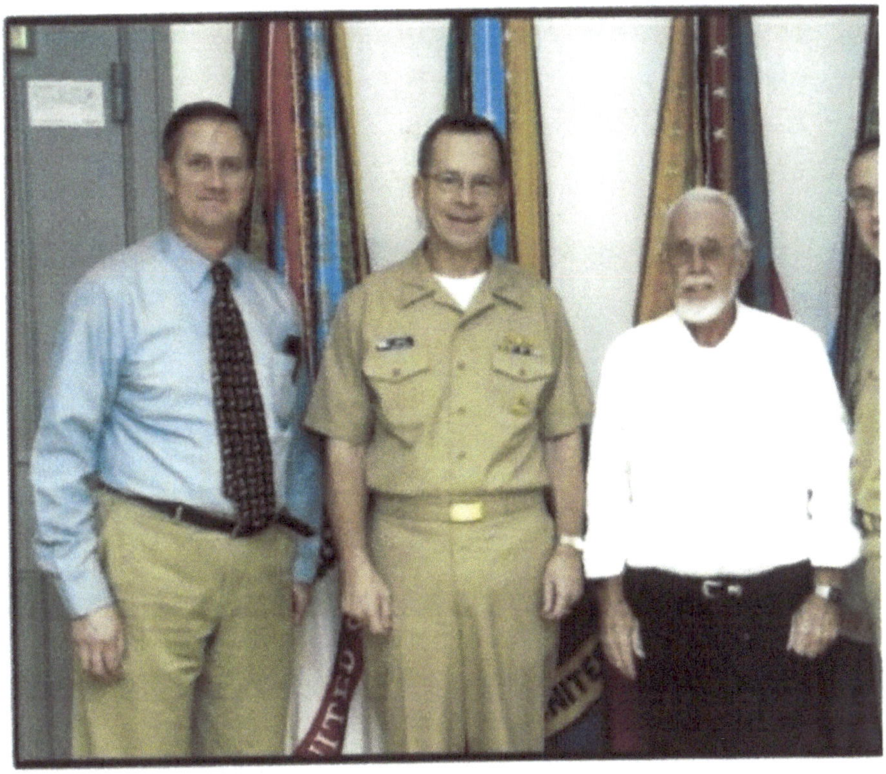

29 January 2008

Eagle's Watch Foundation, Inc.
ATTN: David E. Minyard

Dear Mr. Minyard,

Please accept my sincere appreciation for the selfless work of the Eagle's Watch Foundation. I admire all you do, without fanfare expectation of recognition, to ensure our military members and their families have the opportunity to get a closer view, and a better understanding, of our actions to defend our Nation's freedoms.

Through numerous events, programs, and services, the Eagle's Watch Foundation has brought hope and encouragement to so many. Thank you for making a difference!

With best wishes for continued success,

Sincerely,

PETER PACE
General (Retired)
United States Marine Corps

Chapter 13: 16 November

16 November 2022

Now that it has been made clear that the Town of Viennaism is surely not falling under the US Constitution, not in compliance with the Bill of Rights, and has breached trust with those who are responsible to pay their salaries, each resident that prefers to remain as a part of the United States of America should post a sign, and of the type and construction can be of your choosing, on their own property indicating that anyone wishing to enter the United States of America by coming on their property must show proper identification such as a US Passport to include a drivers license from one of the Native Nations Tribes, one of the 50 States or recognized territories before entering, so in addition to trespassing, they will be considered an illegal alien, and unlike the donkey's, illegal aliens will not be allowed to enter the USA property. Proof of ID will be required. It does not matter if the citizens of Viennaism acknowledge this or not, because the US property falls under the US Constitution and US Bill of Rights and all laws within the State of the residence.

Only one councilmember was bold enough to call out the corruption of the Viennaism council. We will continue to not support sidewalks on Tazewell Road, NW and will not concede to the breach of trust reflected on 14 November 2022.

dave

Guarding and protecting his country, while at the same time, the town where he lives, sells out to corruption, breaches trust, is self-serving, and is the reverse of honoring God and does not support the US Constitution and Bill of Rights.

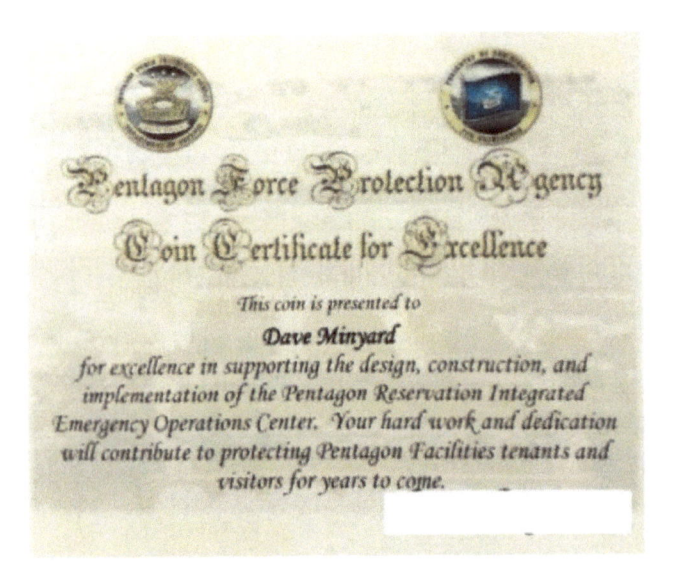

Pentagon Force Protection Agency
Coin Certificate for Excellence

This coin is presented to

Dave Minyard

for excellence in supporting the design, construction, and implementation of the Pentagon Reservation Integrated Emergency Operations Center. Your hard work and dedication will contribute to protecting Pentagon Facilities tenants and visitors for years to come.

Pentagon Memorial Dedication

PENTAGON FORCE PROTECTION AGENCY
AWARD FOR EXCELLENCE

PRESENTED TO

David Minyard

In recognition of your exceptional contributions and efforts surrounding the Pentagon Memorial Dedication Ceremony held on September 11, 2008.

November 2008
DATE

DEPARTMENT OF DEFENSE

WASHINGTON, DC 20301-9000

JUN 0 8

Mr. David E. Minyard

Dear Mr. Minyard:

On February 10, 2015, Secretary Chuck Hagel approved a Joint Meritorious Unit Award (JMUA) for all Office of the Secretary of Defense (OSD) employees, including those working in the Pentagon Force Protection Agency for the period of February 2013 through February 2015. The JMUA is awarded to units in recognition of exceptionally meritorious conduct in the performance of outstanding service. This is the first such award for the Agency, and I am extremely proud, as you should be, of the hard work you have done that resulted in this recognition.

In his memo addressing this award, Secretary Hagel stated, "The last two years have been extremely challenging, especially given all the complex security and personnel issues we have faced as a Department. Everyone has played a part in our success." I agree. Everyone on the PFPA team plays a role in securing and protecting our nation's military headquarters, the facilities that support it and DoD service members and employees. It is noble work.

This award demonstrates that your efforts are appreciated by the Secretary and is deserving of distinction. You should be proud of this accomplishment and your specific contributions to our mission.

Congratulations, and well done!

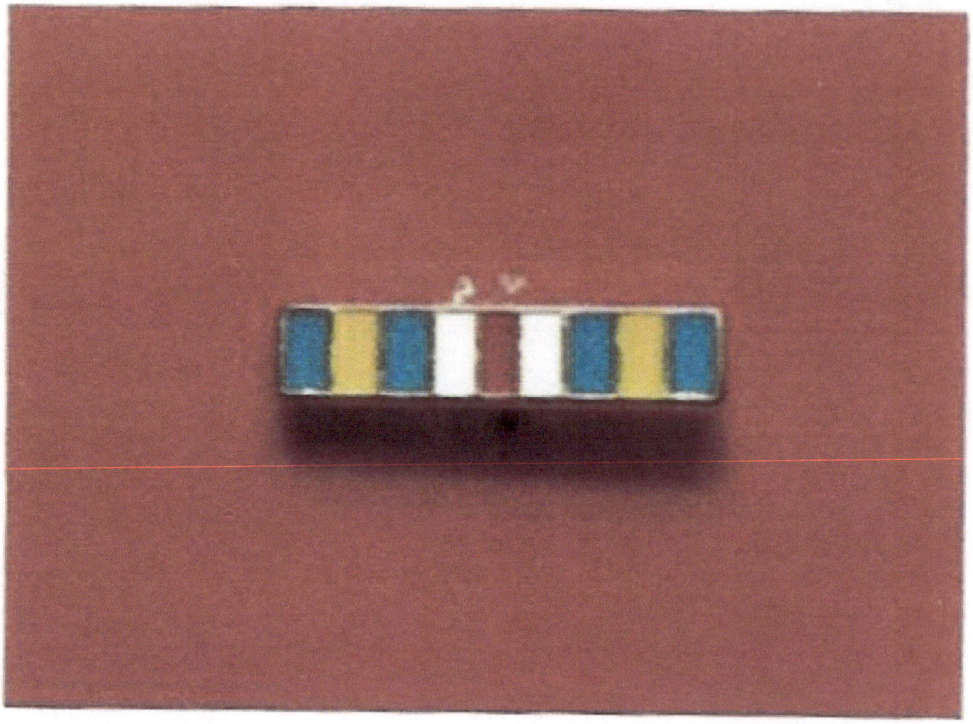

Citation

TO ACCOMPANY THE AWARD OF THE

Joint Meritorious Unit Award

TO THE

Office of the Secretary of Defense

The Office of the Secretary of Defense (OSD) distinguished itself by exceptionally m... achievement from February 2013 to February 2015. During one of the most volatile glob... environments of the last century, OSD civilian and military personnel provided the Se... Defense with an unprecedented level of support. OSD employees provided critical recomm... and took action on a myriad of unpredictable and complex national security issues inc... conclusion of Operation ENDURING FREEDOM in Afghanistan, the transfer of... from the military prison at Guantanamo Bay, the elimination of Syria's chemical weapons... the reassurance of NATO allies and partners in the face of Russian aggression, depl... setting policy for DoD personnel in support of Operation UNITED ASSISTAN... the Ebola virus disease outbreak in West Africa, countering the Islamic State of Ir... Levant through Operation INHERENT RESOLVE, review of the Nuclear... Enterprise, and the continued rebalance of forces towards the Asia-Pacific region. OSD... also championed numerous critical initiatives supporting Service members and their famili... assault prevention and response, suicide prevention, post-traumatic stress and traumatic b... care, and Military Health System reforms top the list of activities by which OSD made... contributions to the health of the force. Throughout this period, the OSD workforce de... superior vision, creativity, competence, and dedication during an era of fiscal uncertaint... constraints, and competing and evolving mission requirements. By their exemplary perf... duty, the men and women of the Office of the Secretary of Defense have brought gre... themselves and to the Department of Defense.

Given under my hand this 10th day of February 2015

Chapter 14: 17 November

17 Nov 2022

It's obvious from Monday night's vote that you all on Council don't care, you aren't concerned with the safety of residents because the Town doesn't vet contractors – no background checks, etc.. So for you each, it is "out of sight, out of mind". You continue to put your head in the sand and drive forward with only your own interests in mind. Those of us who have actually done something to defend this nation and bolstered security that live in the town limits have to add processes in our daily lives now because of that. You'll be responsible for allowing unvetted people to make notes of our routines and patterns if they plan to use that information to engage in criminal activities against any of the residences. What, you didn't think of that? I'm not surprised. In 2000, I was asked to prepare and write a scope of work to bolster the security of the buildings around the US Capitol – Russell Bldg, Hart Bldg, Cannon Bldg, etc., as at the time you could drive right by each of those bldg's. What exists today is a result of that work. You can no longer drive on the side streets adjacent those bldg's with very minor exceptions and there is layered security in place to protect the people and bldg's. Yet here at home, the Town Council is devoid of the reality of this day and age. How short sighted and utterly disgraceful of you. And what about scholarships for kids wanting to pursue college? Your arrogance has created blinders in your eyes and despite the many who walk on streets where there are sidewalks to this day (and yes, not on the sidewalks), you not only have been devoid of common sense and being good stewards of funds, you think that there will be a baseball game on a sidewalk. Wrong. The word politic can be broken down to two words – poli – multiple tics – blood sucking animals – okay, so it's ticks that are the blood sucking animals but phonetic sounds are just as viable to describe the reality of politics. Viennaism it is as defined because of your deeds. What else are you planning on doing to usurp your arrogant position?

Dave

Some in the Town have made a positive difference in protecting our Country yet the Town Council is jeopardizing our safety by bringing in unvetted people to see our daily routines and take notes in case they want to engage in criminal activities. Disgraceful. And you prefer to spend money on useless sidewalks vs divert to scholarships for kids. How self-serving of you.

"Life in Two Lanes", the journey of a person who lived a life that some only thought existed on Action/Adventure Films complete with Stuntmen to do the dangerous stuff. A life that you only thought only James Bond lived in the movies, until now.

Life in Two Lanes

By and about
Dave Minyard

"Life in Two Lanes", the journey of a person who lives a life that some only thought existed on Action/Adventure films complete with Stuntmen to do the dangerous stuff. A life that you thought only James Bond lived in the movies, until now.

Yea, it's an actual book, self-published, you can find it online to purchase throughout the world.

Chapter 15: 18 November

18 Nov 2022

Hmmm what would be more honorable to use money given for scholarships for kids, or for stupid sidewalks where it's statistically seen that even where there are streets with sidewalks, people walk in the streets, walk their dogs in the streets, etc.. So why is it you all are infatuated with sidewalks? Who is driving this? It's abhorrent that tax payers who live on this street and have shown their opposition to this yet you all still in arrogance drove forward and for that, you will never have the respect of myself, nor those who opposed it. You are a disgrace, quite simple. There must be a money trail that is behind this for you all – future aspirations or ambitions with money behind it from those who silently are pushing this maybe? There is always a money trail when politicians fail to represent the people they are supposed to serve. It is the worst type of individual who is two faced – like the councilmen who lied to the neighbors and then let his dog, without being on a leash, do it's "business" in the yard of those who promised that the sidewalk issue would go away, then poof, never talked to them again. You are a corrupt politician and a liar which is obvious. Next? So maybe there will be for sale signs on Tazewell Road? And then you can wish that there would be people to suck up to your fantasy world of you being in control? I heard that JSP Construction CEO, a Conservative minded person, decided against running for Council because of all the so called "progressives" on Council? Well "progressive" another word for woke garbage, like people pushing the jab, when it was all a lie to begin with and actually never was supposed to do anything to prevent Covid 19, but those people pressed it and many in the world bought into the Koolaid.

So what is it you are trying to create here? Your lala land of false joy and community? You have painted the true picture of falsehood and have forgotten the true values that this country was founded upon. "Of the people, by the people, and for the people". Your future Christmas celebrations, Thanksgiving events, are now nothing but your way of creating your fake reality that everything in Vienna is great. In fact, it's Viennaism and it is the complete opposite. And you each are responsible. I am not friends with anyone who are architects of things like this – don't be deceived.

dave

Chapter 16: In closing

There are situations in life, like what the town of viennaism elected (who voted for these self serving people?) folks did that one wants to mark as an awful bunch of people who are all about themselves. It is important not to forget, and going forward, keep watch out for similar dna of those like that in the future.

CPSIA information can be obtained
at www.ICGtesting.com
Printed in the USA
LVHW071836061222
734662LV00016B/672